0

PERSONAL BRANDING

FOR

CAREER AND BUSINESS SUCCESS

DORATHY MASON

INTRODUCTION

The value of having a personal brand will never diminish. In a competitive, constantly evolving workplace, it's actually the only way to stand out and be different. Someone will create a personal brand if you don't have one. You lose control if you allow it to happen, and you might not like the narrative they come up with.

It takes time and effort to stand out from the competition. The majority of people find it difficult to change on their own, so hiring a personal brand coach is an option to think about.

Working with my clients to develop their personal brands as a personal brand coach is my passion. We can collaborate to develop a unique narrative that precisely describes what other people will say when you leave the room, and I find that to be so exciting.

stories from other people.

Spend some time listening to the speakers as they share their personal branding experiences and ideas. Defining who you are and taking charge of your personal and professional lives are both things you will undoubtedly learn a lot about.

Without a doubt, the key to your career success is building a strong personal brand.

Similar to Michelle Obama.

"Your life's story is what you have and always will have,". You should possess it.".

Go ahead and own your story. Set out on a journey to develop your personal brand, which will reflect who you are, your uniqueness, and the value you can bring to the world.

We will discuss the following factors of why personal branding is crucial for business owners.

•Credibility for both your personal and professional brand is increased.

• A personal brand provides you with a platform for expanding your clientele, business opportunities, and income.

• You Have More Freedom and Career Leverage with a Personal Brand.

•Frequently Asked Questions Regarding Why Personal Branding is Important for Entrepreneurs

A personal brand helps you and your business gain credibility.

Executive personal brands are undoubtedly significant and play a part in gaining the trust of their clients at major companies like Microsoft or Apple. However, these corporations can rely on their strong business brands, which have built up reputations and brand loyalty over many years of offering goods and services and are independent of their executives.

Like large corporations, entrepreneurs do not always have the option of relying on well-known brand names. And because many entrepreneurs serve as the public face of their companies, this script is frequently reversed. They are successful in business not because of their company brand but rather because of their personal brand. Customers' perceptions of the business's credibility, trustworthiness, and brand all depend on the entrepreneur in question.

It takes time to develop your own personal brand. It involves a great deal of effort and introspection. Many times, not just once, will you be required to step outside of your comfort zone.

The good news is that you will enjoy being in your comfort zone more the more time you spend there. You can test the viability of and perfect your personal brand when you step outside of your comfort zone.

CHAPTER 1

Here's What Personal Branding Is and Why It's Important:

The importance of personal branding and how to do it correctly are discussed here if you want to be recognized as a reliable authority in your field. Personal branding and its significance in the business world have probably been heavily marketed to you

You might believe that it is just a fad or the product of the marketing gurus' wildest dreams.

Personal branding, however, is a real thing that will only grow more powerful over time.

Let's find out what personal branding is and why it's so crucial.

Why Build Your Own Personal Brand?

Creating a brand identity for a person or a business is called personal branding. The name implies that this is a brand for you or your company.

In essence, it is the manner in which you portray your business to the public and make sure that your target market is aware of who you are, what you stand for, and why they should select you over your competitors.

Being your own marketer is crucial to building your personal brand. You must advocate for yourself and your business if you want to command the respect and trust of your coworkers and clients.

When referring to businesses, the word "branding" can be perceived negatively.

But putting the right ideas into practice will help you distinguish your company from the competition and build a brand identity for it.

A great way to promote yourself and your career to a particular audience or industry is through personal branding. Additionally, it might be extremely beneficial for your career.

Building a personal brand, for example, can give you a competitive advantage over other job candidates who don't have a strong online presence. Alternatively, if you're a businessperson, personal branding could aid in inspiring trust and loyalty in the eyes of potential customers and clients. Politicians and celebrities frequently use this kind of branding strategy to sway the public's perception of them.

Why is personal branding vital?
Making an impression is more crucial than ever in a time when attention spans are decreasing minute by minute. Making a strong and distinctive brand identity is the best way to achieve this.

They believe it involves a lot of extra work, so many business owners do not understand the value of personal branding.

But the fact remains that building a successful brand is a prerequisite for building a successful business.

knowing that people will trust you more and purchase more goods and services from you if they are familiar with you and your company.

Personal branding: 5 justifications
1. Aids in differentiating oneself from the crowd.

In the competitive job market of today, having a strong personal brand is more crucial than ever.

What people think and say about you when you're not around forms your personal brand. Your career may be made or broken by your reputation.

Why is personal branding so crucial, then?

It firstly makes you more noticeable among the crowd.

Employers are looking for candidates with something extra that makes them distinctive in a world where everyone has a degree.

Do you know that you can become the person they remember by creating a strong personal brand?

Personal branding can also enable you to demand a higher salary.

Although there are many ways to build a personal brand, the process begins with understanding who you are and what you want to be recognized for.

Setting yourself up for success in your career and beyond by taking the time to define your brand. The same jobs, clients, and customers are sought after by millions of people in today's digital world, including students and young job seekers. For instance, 57 million of LinkedIn's 810 million users work for employers, according to Kinsta's data.

There is a lot of competition as a result, but recruiters will be interested in candidates with a strong personal brand. Making a lasting impression and standing out from the crowd can be made easier with personal branding.

2) Create opportunities for employment.

A strong personal brand will create opportunities for new employment, speaking engagements, sales leads, etc.

In light of the fact that according to research, 70% of employers screen candidates using social media sites like LinkedIn, this makes perfect sense. Additionally, if you have a strong personal brand, employers are more likely to find you and get in touch with you about job opportunities.

However, if you're a politician, a personal brand can also draw voters, allies, and partners. According to the industry you work in, the opportunities change.

The jobs, clients, and opportunities in our competitive world are sought after by everyone.

It's crucial to have a strong personal brand if you want to stand out from the crowd.

A personal brand is a distinctive mix of abilities and life experiences that define who you are. It is what distinguishes you from others and makes you special.

You can give yourself an advantage over competitors by creating a personal brand.

When people need someone with your specific skills and expertise, they'll think of you and your brand.

In addition, developing a strong personal brand can open up new doors. People are more likely to offer you opportunities to collaborate or work on new projects when they recognize your expertise in the subject matter.

So if you want to advance, start by developing your brand.

want to increase trust, draw in opportunities, or stand out from the crowd.

3. You'll gain the audience's trust.

Making an identity for yourself as a person or a business is known as "personal branding." This entails creating a clear and unified voice, presence, and online and offline brand identity.

You might want to work on your personal brand for a variety of psychology-based reasons.

It can, among other things, aid in the development of audience trust.

Making an identity for yourself as a person or a business is known as "personal branding." This entails creating a clear and unified voice, presence, and online and offline brand identity.

You might want to work on your personal brand for a variety of psychology-based reasons.

It can, among other things, aid in the development of audience trust.

People are more likely to trust you when they feel they know you and what you stand for. This is a result of their perception that you and they are in a relationship.

They are aware of what to expect from you and your status as an expert in your field.

Additionally, personal branding can make you stand out from the competition. Having a strong personal brand can make all the difference in a world where everyone is trying to stand out.

Lastly, developing your personal brand can help you seize opportunities.

Your chances of landing your next project or job increase when potential employers or clients notice that you have a strong personal brand.

Therefore, personal branding might be the solution if you

People are more likely to notice you and have confidence in your work if you have a distinctive personal brand. Additionally, if you brand yourself as an experienced professional, they will naturally trust you more.

When you are acknowledged as an authority in your field, it is much easier to win the trust and confidence of potential clients and consumers.

4. You'll always face online screening.

Personal branding has grown in significance in the digital era.

Anyone can easily learn information about you with a few clicks, thanks to Google and social media. Therefore, it's crucial to be aware of how you come across online.

You can take control of your story and present yourself in the best light by using personal branding. It's a means of differentiating oneself from the competition.

Personal branding can help you distinguish your online presence from those of others in a world where everyone has one.

Gaining the trust of potential clients and customers can also be accomplished through personal branding.

They will be more inclined to do business with you if they can tell that you are an authority in your industry and that you have a strong personal brand.

Anyone who wants to succeed in the modern digital world must, therefore, develop their personal brand.

5) Aids in your goal-achieving.

Your chances of success increase if you match your brand with your objectives. Here are a few illustrations.

•If obtaining employment with a specific organization is your goal, concentrate on developing a personal brand that is consistent with their values and the qualifications they seek in candidates.

• If you are a politician, you want more people to support you and vote for you.

• If your objective is to draw in more clients, concentrate on creating a personal brand that speaks to them and what they want from a company.

A personal brand strategy will be tailored to each person's needs and goals, regardless of the goal..

CHAPTER 2

WHO ARE PERSONAL BRANDS FOR?

Let's start with my personal brand. You are your personal brand. Your abilities, character traits, and values all play a part in it. You are made up of all of these factors combined.

In other words, your personal brand encompasses any impression that people may have of you. There is a well-known statement made by Jeff Bezos, the CEO of Amazon.

"What people say about you when you're not around is your personal brand. ".

the combination of your abilities, characteristics, and values, if you really stop to consider what this means. Each day, in your interactions with others, you exhibit all of these traits. These other people combine all of these "things" to create their impression of you.

When they leave the room, they continue to hold this perception in their heads. From the perspective of your career, this is crucial because how other people perceive you can affect whether or not you are given opportunities.

As a result, your personal brand is crucial in this. Here is an illustration in case you're having trouble understanding this idea.

ASSESSING YOUR PERSONAL BRAND.

For the sake of argument, imagine that you and several of your colleagues are in a conference room. You're all discussing a task or something you're engaged in within the confines of your office. The door opens unexpectedly in the middle of the conversation, and a senior leader sits down at the table.

What happens to the atmosphere, if you will, of that room? Does it remain the same or does it become considerably more somber?

Whatever the result, the senior leader's personal brand has affected the atmosphere in the room.

Consider the same scenario once more. This time, your colleagues are discussing a project at a conference table. This time, when the door opens, you enter.

Does the atmosphere of the room change or does it remain the same at this point?

You must develop self-awareness if you want to know the answer to this question. You'll start to realize what your personal brand is in the eyes of other people once you start to become self-aware.

Knowing who you are as a person will also help you realize the value you bring to the workplace. This calls for a close examination of who you are.

I'll talk more about self-awareness later, but for now, just remember that you are your personal brand. Your traits, skills, and values make you who you are. You are made up of everything.

PHYSICAL BRANDING: WHAT IS IT?

Personal branding is the opposing position. These are the things that I consider to be personal branding.

"The deliberate act of communicating to the world who you are and what value you add. ".

The word **"intentional"** is the key distinction between personal branding and building a personal brand. intentionally establishing your brand in a particular way, ideally in a way that helps people find and recognize your expertise.

You must first know and comprehend what you want to be known for in order to be intentional with your personal branding. It matters whether or not you have a reputation for something. They can only do this if you have made a conscious effort to develop your brand.

People will start to recognize you for what you know if you do this. Even offline, you can brand yourself. Consider your actions and activities in relation to your career when you consider how you behave, speak, dress, and discuss things.

Developing your online brand.

Fortunately, by developing our digital brands, job seekers and career experts can go one step further. In essence, our digital brands are our personal brands online.

However, we deliberately act in a manner that will enable people to find and recognize us for the things we want to become well-known for.

There are many ways we can accomplish this, but having your own website is the best method overall. Having your own website gives you a space online that you can manage; I'll talk more about this later. A location you control where you won't have to worry about the business closing down and taking your data and information with them, as happened recently with the company that branded me.

I believe that a lot of us make unintentional online postings when it comes to digital branding. In many situations, we probably don't even consider the consequences of what we post online or how it might be interpreted by others.

What do you want to be remembered for?

This is a crucial step in developing your online brand. Once you've made a decision about your brand identity, you need to establish it everywhere—online and offline.

In later vlogs, I'll go into this topic a little more, but for now, remember these key points.

You are your own brand. It's everything that makes you, you, including your abilities, characteristics, and values.

Simply put, "personal branding" is the deliberate act of communicating to others who you are and what value you bring. By being deliberate and creating a digital brand that is representative of what we want to become known for, we can take this a step further.

So now that you know, I want you to ask yourself: Are you building the brand for yourself that you want? Are you acting and doing things that will help people understand what you want to be known for?

In fact, I challenge you to spend a few minutes simply deciding what you want to be known for.

What would you want people to say about you when you're not in the room if you could start your career over again?

How to Begin Building Your Brand.

You could start by organizing your social media accounts. Because you have some control over your online reputation, you don't want anything you post on social media to harm it.

A personal website is another excellent place to start.

In addition to helping you build your brand, use your website to assist your audience. You can use this as a platform to highlight your knowledge and expertise while also giving your audience insightful advice.

Make a logo and a theme for yourself, and use them on all of your social media profiles.

Establish your target audience and create a content strategy with them in mind. Create engaging content that will draw in your audience and keep them coming back for more because it adds value to their lives.

A great way to grow your email list is to create specialized, unique content that you can offer your audience in exchange for their email address.

You can have a powerful branding combination that can make it easier and faster for you to achieve your goals when you combine your personal and professional brands.

A decision to think about personal branding can be very beneficial for anyone advancing in their career.

When executed properly, this kind of branding strategy can help you gain more visibility, credibility, and opportunities. The importance of personal branding for your personal and professional lives will now be fully revealed.

Developing a personal branding strategy properly.
It's time to find out how to get started after learning about the benefits of personal branding.

Step 1: Set your primary goals.

Prior to anything else, you must choose precisely what you expect from a personal brand. Once you have a solid understanding of what you want, you can begin working on developing a personal brand that will aid you in achieving your goals.

Step 2: Conduct extensive research.

You now have a clear idea of what you want, so start your research. This step is crucial because it will enable you to comprehend the market's current state and what you must do to stand out.

• The target audience

Delivering what a specific audience wants is where strong personal brands excel. Establish who your main target audiences are before you begin your strategy. The primary objectives you want to accomplish with this personal branding strategy must line up with the target audiences you have chosen, For instance, if you are a musician, your primary target audience will be those who listen to your music and those who enjoy your musical taste. On the other hand, if you are an expert in climate change, your target market might include those looking to learn more about it, potential employers, or other professionals in your industry with whom you might want to collaborate. Give your primary target audiences some thought as you define them and consider their needs. This will enable you to speak in a way that is meaningful to them.

•Competitors.

As with any marketing plan, knowing who your rivals are is essential to being able to position yourself more effectively. You should take the following two actions:

1) List all the individuals or groups that compete with you or share your objectives in order to identify your competitors.

2) Identify what they do and how: Are there major players in your market? What do they have to offer? What are their advantages and disadvantages?

Numerous things are available for you to pick up from your rivals. You'll have a better understanding of what you need to do to stand out if you analyze both your competition and yourself.

- **You personally.**

Your brand has an online and offline presence. Searching for your name on Google should yield some interesting results. Even if nothing occurs, it's not always a bad thing. When people look up your reputation online, you could affect what they find.

Asking your family members' opinions of you and what makes you special in their eyes is another excellent idea.

Finally, examine yourself from your own point of view. What are your abilities, strengths, and areas of expertise that you want to emphasize? How do you want people to see you? What are your weaknesses?

Step 3: Develop a distinctive personal branding strategy.

You are now prepared to create a plan for your personal branding as a result of your previous work. This will serve as your guide for developing and maintaining your brand.

Even though the development of a personal brand is very similar to that of a corporate or organizational brand, they are not the same. The main components of the strategy should be as follows.

- Brand essence: What are your company's goals, objectives, and values?

• Brand positioning or value proposition: What is your company's brand positioning statement, and how are you unique from competitors in your industry? And what products or services can you offer that they don't?

•Brand identity: name, background information, personality traits, visual identity, and communication style.

• Communication strategy: target audience, key media, messaging, and content strategy.

Always keep in mind that you must deliver on your promises to your audience and be consistent with your personal brand across all of your channels. You'll earn your readers' respect and trust by doing this.

What does a personal branding statement mean?

Making a personal branding statement is beneficial when using this kind of strategy. It serves as a way to condense your unique qualities and goals. It should be concise, easy to understand, and straight to the point. It could be regarded as your main pitch.

A personal branding statement is simple to write. Begin by creating a list of your areas of expertise and career goals. Decide on one or two sentences that best describe who you are and what you want to do.

Personal branding statements are frequently found in the bio section of social media profiles, but they are also useful when introducing yourself to different audiences offline.

Examples of personal branding statements.

"I boost businesses' online presence through SEO and content marketing to help them flourish."

and content marketing. I create distinctive WordPress websites in my capacity as a web designer and developer.

I'm an accomplished artist who also appreciates poetry and photography.

These illustrations show that personal branding statements don't have to be intricate or excessive. There ought to be a clear explanation of who you are and what you hope to achieve.

By including a tagline, you can improve your personal branding statement. A catchy phrase that sums up what you do and what makes you unique is called a tagline.

For instance, if your personal branding mission statement reads as follows.

By enhancing businesses' online presence through content marketing and SEO, I help the company grow.

Then this might be your tagline.

"SEO expert that delivers results.".

This tagline and personal branding statement are simple, memorable, and well-written. They succinctly summarize what you do and what sets you apart.

Successful personal branding cases from real life here are some of the most well-known real-world examples of successful personal branding to get you motivated.

The actress Emma Watson, an actress best known for her part in the Harry Potter film series, has worked hard to change how people perceive her as an adult actress who places a strong emphasis on activism. Emma is truly very committed to the feminist cause in addition to her acting career. In order to become a UN woman.

Goodwill Ambassador. She was able to reinvent herself as a strong female leader who pursued education outside of acting. Additionally, she hosted panel discussions for COP26 and promoted eco-friendly fashion. Social responsibility is central to her personal brand and is clearly stated as her purpose.

Tesla Motors. Tesla Motors and SpaceX are just a couple of the companies that Elon Musk founded. Because of his ability to think creatively, he has been compared to "real-life Tony Stark.". His somewhat eccentric nature has contributed to the development of a strong, successful personal brand.

Building a successful career requires strong personal branding. More than just making unique business cards or using pretty fonts, branding yourself and your career involves how you present yourself to potential clients, customers, and other people who are important to your career.

Your brand serves as a showcase for your products or services and has the power to make or break your success. It demonstrates self-assurance, authority, and prioritization skills.

CHAPTER 3

Do you ever wonder how to build a personal brand that is genuine and successful?

Here are three strategies for developing a powerful personal brand that will help you succeed in the workplace!

1. Stay true to who you are.

Even though it may seem obvious, you must put yourself first when developing your personal brand. All that matters is how you appear, speak, and behave. People will take notice of your authenticity when you try to be as true to yourself as you can. They'll usually like what they see, too!

Make sure your voice is clear as well. It's important for your voice to be recognizable, dependable, and consistent. The first thing we did together when I first started assisting Kelly in building his brand was to develop his voice.

You'll be more understood and respected if you develop a message and effectively communicate it to others in a genuine and distinctive way.

2. Pay attention to how you appear online.

If you're unsure of what your online presence looks like, it's time to go through all of your social media and online activities to ensure they align with your brand and present you in the best possible way. During the interview process, 93% of companies claimed they would look up your social media profiles.

Spend some time removing any inaccurate information from the internet and setting up Google alerts for your name so that you are informed whenever new information surfaces. You'll have a better image and, as a result, a more cohesive and expert personal brand, if you stay on top of it and go through those social media feeds with a fine-tooth comb.

3. Sell yourself.

Being personable, relatable, and active on as many social media platforms as you deem appropriate for your brand are all part of personal branding, which is all about effectively marketing yourself. People will relate to and be drawn to your brand if you remind them that you are just as human as they are. Additionally, make sure your narrative is believable, distinctive, and consistent. Your brand will undoubtedly be a success if you concentrate on being yourself online.

Just remember to be yourself, speak up, and put yourself out there because you never know what might happen. If you're like Kelly and you're not sure whether or not you should focus on developing a brand, try to remember that it can help you advance in your career.

Why Personal Branding Is Crucial to Your Career

As a recruiter, I have spoken with and interviewed countless candidates who are unsure of who they are.

Without a personal brand, candidates find it difficult to articulate who they are and how they can benefit the company when asked, "Tell me about yourself—who are you?" You need more than just a resume; a resume by itself won't guarantee you employment.

In essence, your personal brand is essentially your ticket to networking with the right people, getting hired for your dream job, or establishing a powerful business. " She holds that "a strong, proactive proactively of desirable audiences to your vision, abilities, and personality in a way that is in line with your professional objectives"

With just a CV, you wouldn't have been exposed to as many career opportunities as you would have with a personal brand.

What Do You Stand For As A Person?

The job market is extremely competitive and difficult today. Everyone has a CV, but no one else has your unique personal brand, which sets you apart from everyone else and is what people buy—you. A great CV will only get you so far.

The world will remember you for your unique brand. It is how you are viewed by the outside world and the individuals you contact. Your personal brand lasts forever, making it more significant than a business brand as your legacy.

I have coached professionals who have had very successful careers, and they turn to me when they find that they are suddenly not getting the opportunities or having the conversations that would lead them to their next role. They are experiencing a "career meltdown," as I like to call it, and it's all because they lack a personal brand.

A personal brand can assist you in becoming aware of your uniqueness and differences. It enables you to present yourself in a way that sets you apart from the competition, particularly from other candidates for open positions.

Without a doubt, having a strong CV and LinkedIn profile is crucial. To have a CV and LinkedIn profile that is in line with who you are, the value you bring to the market, and your personal guarantee that you deliver There are a few things you need to follow to get results.

In order to build your personal brand, you must present who you are in a strategic, original, and expert manner. Knowing who you are and what you can bring to the table makes it possible for you to be more knowledgeable, flexible, and adaptable to the changing, dynamic workplace. You can prevent having multiple career meltdowns by doing this.

For you to succeed professionally, you must build your personal brand.

The use of social media by recruiters during the interview process is more common, which is one of the causes. A 2018 CareerBuilder survey found that 43% of employers use social media to check in on current employees and

70% of employers use social media to screen candidates during the hiring process. ".

Looking someone up on LinkedIn or other social media sites like Facebook, Instagram, and Twitter is the first thing I do as a recruiter when I want to research a candidate or coach a client. Your digital footprint is the window through which the rest of the world can see who you are. When you let other people judge who you are for you because you have no control over how you want to be perceived, you are seriously misjudging yourself.

"Your brand is what people say about you when you are not in the room," stated Jeff Bezos, the founder of Amazon, at one point. "Believe me "If you don't have personal branding, others will define you quickly and erroneously."

You are in charge when you have a personal brand. When you leave the room, you are completely aware of what will be said about you.

This is demonstrated by the personal brand of well-known businessman Gary Vaynerchuk. Great services are offered to customers by his businesses, such as his marketing firm VaynerMedia.

The thing that distinguishes Vaynerchuk's business from the competition and attracts top brands to work with him is his well-known personality and reputation as an innovator and thought leader. With his strong work ethic, openness, and approachability on display, Vaynerchuk has built an engaged community and a personal brand that attracts customers, staff members, and business partners.

This kind of impact elevates personal branding from a nice-to-have—as it might be with other career paths—to an indispensable asset that is directly related to revenue and business ROI. As a result, personal branding becomes the primary marketing channel for entrepreneurs.

For entrepreneurs, income and reputation are correlated.

The more money you can charge for your goods and services and the better clients you can work with, the stronger your personal brand will be.

For instance, Niharikaa Kaur Sodhi is now regarded as a top author on websites like LinkedIn, Twitter, and Medium. She is able to charge competitive rates for both her consulting services and digital goods. When she first started out, she couldn't be picky about the writers she worked with or the writing jobs she accepted, as she writes in her personal branding content. Her expertise is in high demand, so as her brand grew, she was able to draw higher-paying clients.

By enhancing their personal brands and raising the bar for their reputations, all business owners can follow in this person's footsteps. Depending on how they want to spend their time, they will be able to charge more and sell more or less as their reputation grows.

Referrals: Whether you pursue an opportunity or the opportunity pursues you depends on your personal brand.

You will not only be able to work with higher caliber and better-paying clients and customers, but you will also be able to find them more readily as your personal brand gains credibility.

This is due to the role that a personal brand plays in driving business referrals. Word will get out, and referrals from people in your niche will start coming in as you continue to build a following that trusts you and provide more customers and clients with positive experiences.

People Want to Buy From People They Can Trust.

People are purchasing more and more from trusted individuals in the era of influencers, key opinion leaders (KOLs), and creator brands. Consumers are thought to be interested in purchasing goods that are regarded as credible by respected experts in their respective fields. And consumers are reacting: 74 percent of consumers claim that word-of-mouth influences their purchasing decisions.

One of our favorite personal brands to discuss, for instance, is Erika Kullbergs. In the legal sector, she has established a strong personal brand. On websites like Facebook, YouTube, and TikTok, Kullberg shares legal advice and tips with her sizable fan base. She also sells templates for common legal document requirements through her company, Plug, and Law.

Despite the fact that her products are excellent, she still receives business because of her well-known personal brand and the authority she has built during her successful legal career. She has been able to transfer that same trust and credibility to her business by providing so much free value to people through her personal brand channels and developing trust with her audience.

People will buy from businesses just as much for their own brands as they will for the leaders of those businesses, so entrepreneurs who develop strong personal brands can benefit from this trend in consumer purchasing.

individual and corporate brands combining.

When contrasting personal brands vs. business brands We discussed how personal and corporate brands are merging. Creators like Kullberg and others who have equated their personal brands with their businesses are the ones who are driving this trend.

Many business owners are developing their companies under their own brand names rather than creating separate brands for each, as Jeff Bezos did with Amazon. For instance, Justin Welsh is a "solopreneur" who aims to amass a portfolio of small businesses that collectively generate $5 million in annual revenue. In order to generate client and customer leads, he developed his own line of goods and services as well as a multi-channel marketing funnel.

As entrepreneurs continue to experience success with personal branding-driven growth, expect this trend to persist.

You can diversify your audience, business opportunities, and income with the help of a personal brand.

One of the biggest advantages of personal branding is that it will serve you well for the duration of your career.

Professionals can use their personal brand to advance their careers and find new employment by bringing it with them from job to job. A personal brand can even assist professionals in changing their career trajectory by starting to work for themselves and leaving their 9–5 jobs if it is monetized through side businesses.

You can use your personal brand as a launchpad for new businesses if you are an established entrepreneur who is currently self-employed or working as a part-time creator.

Examples of Entrepreneurs Who Use Their Personal Brand as a Launchpad for New Businesses and Income Streams.

One well-known illustration of this is Gary Vaynerchuk. When he was in charge of his family's wine and liquor company, Vaynerchuk began building his own personal brand. He rose to prominence and earned the title of marketing guru by disclosing the marketing and business strategies he was employing to grow his family's company to $60M in revenue. That naturally inspired him to launch his marketing and advertising firm, VaynerMedia. From there, Vaynerchuk used his established personal brand to sell books, accept speaking engagements for payment, and launch a number of other companies, including VaynerSports, an agency for professional athletes.

Following a similar strategy, Justin Welsh has expanded the range of goods and services he offers as his personal brand has developed. By selling digital goods like courses and ebooks, he expanded his business beyond consulting.

As your personal brand develops, opening new ventures and sources of income will become simpler.

Launching new companies and products will become simpler over time as you build an established following and reputation to support them, similar to how building an audience on a new platform is easier when you already have an audience on another platform.

You can introduce more goods, services, and ventures as your personal brand develops and your niche audience grows as a result of adding new subjects in which you are well-known and corresponding audience segments.

By treating your personal brand like a platform, you can use it as a tool to earn money and establish your thought leadership throughout the rest of your career.

More freedom and professional sway are yours with a personal brand.

The freedom it grants you is a personal, and possibly even more potent, reason why personal branding is important for entrepreneurs.

A personal brand is frequently referred to as a "career safety net" when discussing its importance. This is because having a strong personal brand ensures financial security for you no matter what circumstances arise.

For instance, if your personal brand has developed to the point where it is generating leads from high-quality clients and allowing you to charge more for goods and services, you can decide to work fewer hours if you'd like and embrace a work-life balance. Alternatively, you can continue to put in as many hours as you like to grow your company.

Professionals with no personal brand or smaller personal brands have a different level of career leverage than those with this level. They lack a solid reputation and passive income streams to fall back on if they stop working hard or lose their job from an employer.

Therefore, one of the biggest advantages of personal branding is the freedom it allows in one's life and career. The ability to choose what you want to work on and when you want to work on it comes from building a strong personal brand.

CHAPTER 4

Final Thoughts on Why Personal Branding Is Important for Entrepreneurs.

Any professional can greatly benefit from having a personal brand, but entrepreneurs in particular. Entrepreneurs have never had a better reason to invest in personal branding than they do now, as personal and business brands increasingly overlap, consumers pay more attention to the people they are buying from, and professionals are creating more often outside of their day jobs. We hope the research, advice, and case studies in this blog post will help you establish your own distinctive brand and accomplish your entrepreneurial objectives.

Answers to Frequently Asked Questions About Why Personal Branding is Important for Entrepreneurs.

How does personal branding help entrepreneurs?

Personal branding is beneficial for entrepreneurs because it gives them a platform to boost their company's reputation, draw in more customers of a higher caliber, and expand their sources of income.

Why is personal branding advantageous?

In addition to increasing your network and opening up career opportunities, personal branding also gives you the chance to make money through hustles and entrepreneurship.

How vital is personal branding to career success?

Personal branding is crucial for career success because it develops an asset that shows your credibility, showcases and enhances your skill set, and broadens your network, opening up more opportunities for employment and business ventures.

Why do business owners need personal brands?

Because they serve as the public face of their companies, entrepreneurs need personal brands because they frequently lack the kind of strong corporate brand that a big, well-known company can use to its advantage in marketing. This means that for their companies to expand and build a solid reputation, entrepreneurs must build their brands and rely on them.

Building a personal brand has never been more crucial for freelancers and business owners. Anyone with internet and social media access has the ability to establish a following, establish expertise, and begin luring customers to their business. and many individuals are doing just that.

According to an Upwork study, the U.S. workforce as a whole is growing at a rate 3x slower than that of the freelance workforce. Freelancers are anticipated to make up the majority of the U.S. workforce by 2027. S. workforce.

Although it's encouraging to see so many people embracing their entrepreneurial spirit, this also means that there will soon be more competition for independent contractors, freelancers, and business owners than there is now. Building a personal brand is the key to standing out from the competition.

Why every business owner needs to develop their personal brand

When developing a company around your niche (as an author, speaker, coach, consultant, freelancer, etc.), the idea of creating a personal brand probably sounds familiar to you. Building your personal brand is a no-brainer when you are the public face of your company.

What sets you apart from your rivals is your brand, which also aids in leaving a positive impression on your target audience and clients. You might find it difficult to create a successful and long-lasting business without a compelling personal brand that draws in your target market.

Building a personal brand has advantages even if you are developing a business with its own brand (a software or physical product company, for example).

The majority of people are more likely to follow other people than they are to follow particular businesses. Building a following for your personal brand can therefore help your business get more exposure.

For instance, Elon Musk has more Twitter followers than all three of his businesses put together (SpaceX, Tesla, and SolarCity). The same is true for many other wildly successful businesspeople, including Richard Branson (Virgin), Arianna Huffington (Thrive Global), Gary Vaynerchuck (VaynerMedia), and countless others. They all have potent personal brands that they use to broaden their visibility and draw in more clients for their businesses.

Building a personal brand and a company brand does not have to be mutually exclusive. Both can be constructed simultaneously. Personal branding.

As CEOs and founders of companies/brands must now stand out and interact with their audiences more than ever, having a personal brand is essential for entrepreneurs. "People have relationships.".

The benefits of developing a personal brand include

• Trust and authority: Having a personal brand position you as an authority and thought leader in your industry and helps you develop trust with your audience.

• Get media attention: You may more easily pitch and be noticed by the media if you have a personal brand (online publications, magazines, television, radio, podcasts, etc.). The media is always looking for specialists who can share their knowledge with their audience.

•Create a network: It's easier for other people to relate to you when you have a personal brand that concisely describes who you are, what you do, and how you help others. people and business owners to see the benefit of getting in touch with you. You can quickly and efficiently expand your network both online and offline by utilizing your personal brand.

- **Attract more clients:** Developing a personal brand that establishes you as the authority in a particular sector or market enables you to draw in more of your ideal clients. It's also easier for people to recommend clients to you when you're seen as an authority figure.

- **Premium pricing:** A powerful personal brand makes it acceptable to charge a premium for your goods and services. Without a brand, you turn into a commodity that competes on price. Additionally, there will always be rivals who can undercut your price.

- **Build a solid foundation:**

As your company grows, so will its platform. Throughout your career, you might even launch a number of companies in various sectors. As you transition from one business venture to another, your personal brand follows you.

A brand that connects to a person's face is much easier to trust faster because there is so much content and so many small businesses emerging online. Building a relationship with a personal brand is quicker and easier than with a corporate brand. ".

How to Build a Successful Personal Brand in Social Media

We've outlined 7 specific steps to help you develop a compelling (and lucrative!) personal brand that draws in your ideal customers after speaking with dozens of business owners and branding specialists.

As you read through these steps, you can use our fillable Personal Branding Workbook to help you develop your personal brand strategy.

1. Lay a solid foundation.

Laying a solid foundation upon which to confidently and authentically build your personal brand is the first step. Authenticity is the main idea here.

It's a common misconception that developing a personal brand entails creating a persona. However, a persona is a facade by nature. It is inauthentic because it is not a true representation of who you are.

You shouldn't use your personal brand to give a misleading image of who you are. When it comes to branding, it's not about pretending to be someone you're not. It's about presenting your true self to your audience and clients in a deliberate and strategic way. Your personal brand should appropriately represent your abilities, passions, values, and beliefs.

Make a list of the current resources for your brand.

Beginning by making a list of the branding assets you already have will help you lay a solid brand foundation. You should develop your personal brand at the point where these assets intersect.

•Your qualifications: What training, degrees, certifications, or honors have you received? What skills have you acquired over the course of your life?

•Your interests.

Core values.

The following are important building blocks for your personal branding strategy.

The next step is to begin putting the pieces of your personal brand together after you have determined your current brand assets. As you develop your personal brand, these will support your decision-making.

• Your brand vision: If you were the world's foremost authority on XYZ subject, what would you want to be known for?

•Your brand mission: What is your motivation for creating a personal brand, whom are you trying to influence, and what are you hoping to achieve?

• Your brand message: What is the main idea you want to get across? What message do you want to consistently reaffirm in your content and marketing? If you could only offer your audience one piece of advice, what would it be?

• Your brand personality: What are some of your personal qualities and traits that you can incorporate into your image? Do you want to come across as very polished and businesslike, or perhaps more eccentric and daring?

2. Decide whom you want to reach.

Making the mistake of attempting to appeal to everyone is one of the worst things you can do when developing your personal brand. Not everyone is your ideal client, though.

You must be willing to turn away potential clients that you do not want to work with in order to draw in your ideal customers. This entails determining a particular target market and creating an alluring brand for them.

Even though it goes against common sense, trying to win everyone's affection will make you unpopular. In order to be noticed, you must be divisive. It's okay if not everyone who hears or sees your message and connects with you. To create a successful business, you don't have to appeal to everyone. You just need to find your ideal clients.

"You must stand for something, have beliefs that are obvious, and freely express those ideas from your platform if you want to build a powerful personal brand." Companies who fail to accomplish this encounter a poor reaction from their target markets and wonder why their efforts have failed to motivate them to take action.

Making your ideal client profile, also known as a client avatar, is a worthwhile exercise that we advise doing. You'll be better equipped to develop goods and services that your ideal client really wants and needs if you have a better understanding of everything about them, including their needs and difficulties.

You can use the following inquiries to create your ideal client profile.

•Demographics, including age, gender, education, marital status, income, and occupation;

•Desires and aspirations: What is the person's ideal future? What are their hopes and objectives?

•Pain points and challenges: what are they battling, and what is getting in the way of their objectives?

3. Make a compelling offer.

You must have a product to sell to your target market in order to develop a successful personal brand. You need a compelling offer that assists your target market in resolving a particular issue or achieving a particular objective.

Many business owners make the mistake of producing a good or service that they would like to use, only to find that no one else does or would be willing to pay for it.

In light of this, it is crucial to identify your ideal customer before developing a product or service. You can create an offer that is the ideal solution for someone when you are clear about whom you want to assist.

How to come up with a deal that your customers will adore.

Positioning yourself as a specialist and not a generalist is the first step in developing an irresistible offer. Make a very specific outcome promise to your clients and create a tailored offer to assist them in achieving that promise. Uncompelling is not a generic offer with a hazy promise.

Find the points where your passion, expertise, and the needs of your ideal clients overlap next. Then make a proposal that satisfies both of these requirements. The "Irresistible Offer"

The Formula for an Irresistible Offer

What you love to do, what you excel at, and what your audience most desires combine to make an irresistible offer.

You must be able to clearly communicate your irresistible offer to your audience once you have one. The following two questions require that you be able to respond succinctly and clearly.

Your value proposition can be summed up as simply as "What do you do?" you must endeavor to your customer gets value for the money they give you

Give the name of your procedure, item, or service a distinctive sound. Giving it a distinctive name makes it stand out from rival offers that make the same promise.

For instance, Nicholas Kusmich, a Facebook advertising strategist, assists businesses in quickly scaling their revenue by attracting more customers through Facebook advertising. He does that. He created a proprietary process and gave it the distinctive name "Contextual Congruence" to help him stand out from the thousands of other Facebook advertising experts who perform the same task.

The following is a screenshot from the home page of his website, which highlights how he stands out from his rivals by describing what he does.

In the simplest terms possible, you must let people know who you are and what you do. Ensure simplicity. Your brand should be able to be expressed in no more than five words. ".

4. Personalize your website.

Building a personal brand requires many different elements, one of which is having a personal website. Although having a significant social media presence is important, you do not own or have any control over the social platforms where you choose to do so. Your website is a platform that you own and have control over, and frequently, a target audience will take your website as one of the first steps on their path to becoming a customer.

The importance of first impressions. When your target audience visits your personal website, they should be able to tell right away who you are and how you can help them. They ought to feel as though they have arrived in the appropriate place. The majority of new visitors will leave your website if this doesn't happen within a few seconds.

More importantly, your website should be optimized to turn inactive visitors into active customers. Making this happen requires a number of essential components, the majority of which belong right on your homepage.

important components of your website's home page.

Hire a designer to transform your name into a professional logo. On this page, we offer a list of some of the best online business tools if you're looking for a graphic design service.

Make sure your value proposition—whom you help and how—is prominently displayed on your homepage, ideally near the top.

Get yourself several pictures taken by a professional photographer. Utilize these pictures for your social media profiles and the entirety of your website.

Add the logos of any publications or media outlets in which you have been featured, as well as client or customer testimonials for social proof (media).

A clear call to action: Provide your website, and visitors, with a clear next step, such as signing up for your email list, attending a free webinar, or requesting a free consultation.

Our friend Jeanine Blackwell's website is among the best illustrations of a personal brand. Here is a screenshot of the home page of her website, which includes every aspect listed above.

Additional crucial pages for a personal brand website include

Here are some additional key pages that your personal brand website should have in addition to your homepage.

Describe yourself on the About page. What qualifications and experience do you have? Whom do you assist? How do you assist them? Why do you do what you do?

Chris Ducker's website is a good place to start if you want to see an example of a well-written About Page. Here is a screenshot from his About Page, where he tells his personal story in just one section.

Make it simple for website visitors to convert to customers or clients by offering them your products or services. List any sales-oriented products, programs, or services you offer, along with links to information about them or places to buy them (depending on how you approach sales for each).

Free resources and/or content include blog posts, podcast episodes, instructional videos, and lists of resources you have compiled or suggested.

Provide a clear method of contact on your website's contact page. Give them various ways to get in touch with you (email, social media, etc.) based on the reason they are getting in touch with you.

Lewis Howes has one of the best contact pages we've come across. He has established many contact forms for various sorts of questions in an effort to manage incoming contact requests.

You need to build a brand that is entirely focused on you before you can profit from your own "blue ocean," which is a market where you can operate in an uncontested region. Due to the fact that none of your competitors can replicate or clone everything that makes you unique and exclusive, this environment is free from traditional competitive dynamics.

5. A content strategy is necessary.

One of the best ways to establish your brand and win the confidence of your target audience is to produce and distribute free content. You create content that actually helps your audience, rather than attempting to persuade them that you can help them. By doing this, you increase trust and establish yourself as an authority in your field.

It is no accident that the top personal brands of today—Grant Cardone, Marie Forleo, and Gary Vaynerchuck, to name a few—publish a sizable amount of content online to support audience development.

Start by making a list of all the potential topics that would be beneficial for your target audience in order to develop a content strategy for your personal brand. Three excellent resources for conducting keyword research and identifying trending topics are BuzzSumo, Answer the Public, and Google's Keyword Planner.

The next step is to choose which type of content to produce and where to publish it once you have a list of topics for your content.

Typical content types are:

• Text and/or articles

•Videos.

•Podcasts.

•Webinars.

Online courses.

• Worksheets, checklists, and guides in PDF format

•Infographics.

•Slideshows.

•Case analyses.

Common content delivery methods include

• Your own website or blog

• Directories of podcasts (such as iTunes, Stitcher, etc.

•YouTube.

Alternative blogs and online publications.

Social media platforms like Facebook, LinkedIn, etc

•Email.

•Slideshare.

•Quora.

Build a series of content around some central ideas in which you firmly believe and then keep hammering them home. ".

Pay attention to consistency and quality.

Quality and consistency must be the main priorities in content marketing for it to be effective. Avoid publishing content that will damage your brand, and be reliable in how frequently you update your audience with fresh material. When done properly, content marketing is a long-term strategy that yields incredible returns.

Most people don't realize how much time and money goes into creating and promoting content. For this reason, we advise beginning with 1-2 primary content types (like blog posts or videos) and 1-2 primary content platforms (like YouTube - for more information, check out the YouTube Marketing Guide or Facebook). Expand into other content types and mediums once you've begun seeing success with your primary ones in order to reach a larger audience.

Check out our comprehensive guide to producing epic content that your customers will love to learn more about how to produce high-quality content.

A powerful personal brand is consistent, honest, and serves a defined target. The best approach for an entrepreneur to communicate their authentic message is through their own brand and attract their target audience.

6. Develop a visibility plan.

It takes a lot of time to build an audience by publishing content on your own platforms, though. Exposure to other people's audiences can help you expand your audience more quickly.

These are a few typical methods for enhancing your visibility.

•Interviews

•Guest blogging: Create content for blogs and websites read by your target audience.

• Public speaking: submit applications to present at conferences, live events, and neighborhood Meetup groups that your target audience frequents.

•Partnerships

Getting your name in prominent publications is the single best growth hack. What better way to establish authority and credibility within your niche than to have one of the most prestigious brands mention you?

7. Establish a community.

Focus on leading a community in a particular niche rather than trying to build a sizable and diverse audience. Create a community for your target audience so they can interact with one another, share ideas, support one another, and get in touch with you. Define your target audience.

Here are a few strategies for creating a community around your name and company.

•Facebook Groups: Establish a closed Facebook group for your viewers or clients. This will give you the chance to have daily meaningful conversations with your audience and, more importantly, it will create an atmosphere where they can interact with and support one another.

and get in touch with you. Define your target audience.

Here are a few strategies for creating a community around your name and company.

•**Facebook Groups:**

 Establish a closed Facebook group for your viewers or clients. This will give you the chance to have daily meaningful conversations with your audience and, more importantly, it will create an atmosphere where they can interact with and support one another.

•**Live**

Events: Hold live events so that you can interact in person with your audience and/or clients. There are many effective ways to build enduring relationships with your audience, including casual meetups, exclusive dinners, workshops, retreats, and mastermind groups.

•**Membership Sites:**

Set up a membership website where, in return for a small monthly fee, your customers can access exclusive content, participate in regularly scheduled live calls and/or webinars with you, and engage in private forums or groups.

"A strong personal brand is one that makes a significant impact, which then results in influence among your followers." Utilizing social media and other online communities is key to starting meaningful conversations with the people you want to have an impact on.

Develop your personal brand by starting now.

A better time has never existed for starting a business. The internet and technology have made it so that starting a business has virtually no entry requirements. Anyone can create a brand, an audience, and products and services to sell to that audience online.

You have rivals if you're a freelancer or business owner. But you don't have a personal brand. There is no true competition when developing your personal brand. Sure, there may be other people and businesses selling comparable goods and services to yours, but they are not you. In actuality, no one else in the entire world is exactly like you. You are a singular person, with no two like you.

For this reason, developing a personal brand is so effective. Because YOU are unique compared to your competitors, when you develop a personal brand, you stand out from the crowd.

Whether or not we recognize it, each of us has a unique brand. So let's do it on purpose. My definition of a strong brand is the ability to recognize your message. The perception of competition is reduced when you are known for something. That is significant.

LinkedIn is one of the biggest social networking sites for organizations and professionals, with over 810 million members. How can leaders grow their personal brands on LinkedIn? Lead generation outperforms Facebook and Twitter by 277 percent.

LinkedIn's goal is to boost your professional reputation while also attracting customers to your brand. Utilize the platform's features and tools to the fullest extent possible to participate actively. You can use a variety of strategies to expand your personal brand on LinkedIn. Here are five of them for leaders who are in place or who want to be.

1. Build a profile that is captivating.

Make sure your profile is distinct and professional-looking before doing anything else. It's amazing how many people skip this step and then wonder why their social presence isn't increasing.

First impressions matter, and if a prospective client or customer doesn't like what they see, they will move on to the next person they find similarly situated. Concerning outreach, the same is true.

Having said that, start by taking a crisp headshot for your profile picture before writing your bio. Your visitors will get a sense of your brand's mission from your bio if it is well-written and clearly describes what you do at your current job. Your bio should serve as a hook to pique the reader's interest and persuade them that you can deliver the service they need.

2. Improve your individual page.

People are less likely to connect with you on LinkedIn if they are unaware that you exist.

Your chances of being found on LinkedIn will rise if you optimize your page. If you want to use LinkedIn to the fullest extent possible, you should treat it like a search engine.

According to research, less than 6% of searchers click on the second page. And LinkedIn is the same. If a client is looking for a graphic designer, they will type the appropriate keywords into the search bar and interact with the profiles on the first page of the results. Your page should appear in that location.

It won't happen overnight, but you can move up the relevant search results rankings. Here are some pointers for improving your profile so it has a better chance of appearing on the front page.

Create a complete profile.

• Include a catchy headline.

• Include the pertinent keywords.

• Complete the "about" section.

• Insert your location.

• Be detailed in your descriptions of the goods and services you offer.

3. Become a participant who is active.

Your LinkedIn profile won't help you if it is inactive. It won't suffice to simply post your LinkedIn profile and hope for the best. You must put in the necessary effort if you want your brand to grow.

One of the most effective growth strategies is to offer value. You can achieve this by offering your audience educational and interesting content. Write about hot topics in your field along with strange, esoteric subjects that will spark discussion.

Your writing will help you position yourself as a thought leader in your field and provide your audience with more information about who you are.

4. Connect with the Right Group of People

Just as you wouldn't go to a chance networking event that wouldn't help you, don't connect with everyone on LinkedIn.

Connecting with businesses and people in your industry who have active profiles is the key to effective LinkedIn networking. You can conduct much of your networking from the comfort of your home thanks to the website's industry-specific online events. Connect with the event organizers and attendees.

Additionally useful as a tool for networking are LinkedIn Groups. By participating in these groups, you can connect with business people who can help elevate your brand.

5. Obtain excellent endorsements.

Although having a stellar resume is ideal, anyone can list their qualifications. The opinions of others are more significant than your own.

The platform for endorsements on LinkedIn is a crucial component. It enables your clients to vouch for the abilities you've emphasized. Your social proof becomes more credible as you accrue more endorsements. So don't be afraid to ask clients who have used your services to recommend you.

The platform should be used for at least an hour every day, according to experts. Create a plan, choose the areas you want to concentrate on, and stick to it. You will soon begin to notice significant growth and brand exposure on LinkedIn if you take this action.

CONCLUSION

A business is nothing without a personal brand behind it
.however, this does not mean you must forsake your business
for your brand. Instead, it would be best to have a clear and
purposeful strategy for the two.

Personal branding can only be successful if backed by a
strong business strategy

.If your plan is weak, your brand is already defeated before it
has even begun.

www.ingramcontent.com/pod-product-compliance
Lightning Source LLC
Chambersburg PA
CBHW071050220526
45467CB00004B/1756